So You Think You

PORTSMOUTH

A QUIZ & MISCELLANY

THE FRANCIS FRITH COLLECTION

www.francisfrith.co.uk

CW01655263

First published in the United Kingdom in 2005 by The Francis Frith Collection®

Hardback edition published in 2005 ISBN 1-84589-246-1

Text and Design copyright The Francis Frith Collection®
Photographs copyright The Francis Frith Collection® except where indicated.

The Frith® photographs and the Frith® logo are reproduced under licence from Heritage Photographic Resources Ltd, the owners of the Frith® archive and trademarks.
'The Francis Frith Collection', 'Francis Frith' and 'Frith' are registered trademarks of Heritage Photographic Resources Ltd.

All rights reserved. No photograph in this publication may be sold to a third party other than in the original form of this publication, or framed for sale to a third party. No parts of this publication may be reproduced, stored in a retrieval system, or transmitted, in any form, or by any means, electronic, mechanical, photocopying, recording or otherwise, without the prior permission of the publishers and copyright holder.

British Library Cataloguing in Publication Data

So You Think You Know? Portsmouth
Text adapted from original material supplied by Sarah Quail

The Francis Frith Collection
Frith's Barn, Teffont,
Salisbury, Wiltshire SP3 5QP
Tel: +44 (0) 1722 716 376
Email: info@francisfrith.co.uk
www.francisfrith.co.uk

Printed and bound in England

Front Cover: **PORTSMOUTH, TRAMS AT CLARENCE PIER** ZZZ04520t (Portsmouth City Museums and Records Service)

The colour-tinting is for illustrative purposes only, and is not intended to be historically accurate

Aerial photographs reproduced under licence from Simmons Aerofilms Limited.

Modern (2005) images by Sarah Quail unless otherwise specified.

Every attempt has been made to contact copyright holders of illustrative material.
We will be happy to give full acknowledgement in future editions for any items not credited.
Any information should be directed to The Francis Frith Collection.

AS WITH ANY HISTORICAL DATABASE, THE FRANCIS FRITH ARCHIVE IS CONSTANTLY BEING CORRECTED AND IMPROVED, AND THE PUBLISHERS WOULD WELCOME INFORMATION ON OMISSIONS OR INACCURACIES

CONTENTS

PORTSMOUTH, PUBLIC ART, WYMERING COMMUNITY CENTRE 2005 P100707k

PORTSMOUTH MISCELLANY

The original Portsmouth was probably at the top of Portsmouth harbour, at the entrance to Fareham Creek.

The first English naval battle may well have taken place at the top of Portsmouth harbour in AD 896, between King Alfred's ships and six Viking boats.

The remains of a small Saxon boat were discovered in the mud at the top of Langstone Harbour in 2003.

The early history of Portsmouth is recorded in the Southwick Cartularies, the collection of documents relating to gifts made to Southwick Priory from its foundation.

Portsmouth's founder, Jean de Gisors, features in Dan Brown's blockbuster novel 'The Da Vinci Code' - as a member of the Order of Sion. There is no foundation to this particular part of the story.

Southwick Priory was established originally within the confines of Portchester Castle by Henry I in the 1120s. The canons moved over the hill to the village of Southwick in the mid 12th century.

Portsmouth's parish church is dedicated to St Thomas of Canterbury, not St Thomas the Apostle.

Richard I built a house for himself in Portsmouth. It was known as the King's House and occupied a site at the top of Penny Street, now part of Portsmouth Grammar School. The area was known as Kingshall Green until at least the 19th century.

There are references to a borough council, the predecessor of today's city council, as early as the 1230s.

According to the earliest local by-laws, the 'Customs and Usages', thieves had their ears nailed to the pillory in early medieval Portsmouth and scolds were immersed in the Camber on the ducking stool.

PORTSMOUTH
THE OLD MUNICIPAL COLLEGE
2005 P100711k

SOUTHSEA, DAGMAR TERRACE 1890 22764

Portsmouth was raided by the French on at least four occasions during the Hundred Years' War.

The Garrison Church was a medieval hospice known as the Domus Dei, or God's House. From before the Reformation, it provided accommodation for pilgrims and strangers and cared for local people who needed nursing.

The first defences went up round Portsmouth in the late 14th century - an earthwork round the town itself and a tower, the precursor of the Round Tower, at the harbour entrance.

The people of Portsmouth were excommunicated in 1450 for the murder of the Bishop of Chichester within the precincts of the Domus Dei. It was said at the time that he was set upon by soldiers and sailors, aggrieved that they had not been paid their wages, but it was more likely a political assassination, procured by enemies of the king, Henry VI. Whatever the truth of the matter the church held Portsmouth and all its people responsible.

SOUTHSEA, THE SEAFRONT 1892 30018

After the people of Portsmouth were excommunicated following the murder of the Bishop of Chichester in the town, they were not admitted back into the church until 1508, and only then after a most elaborate ceremony, during which the mayor and other leading townsfolk had to make their way on their knees from the Domus Dei, where the bishop was murdered, to the parish church, wearing penitential clothes.

Richard I built the first bridge over Portscreek. Henry VIII had the first bulwark constructed there to defend the crossing.

The remains of a member of the ship's crew of the 'Mary Rose' were interred in the Cathedral on 19 July 1984.

The house where the Duke of Buckingham was assassinated in 1628 still stands at the top of the High Street. It is called 'Buckingham House'.

A fine monument to the Duke of Buckingham, erected by his sister, stands in St Thomas's Church.

PORTSMOUTH, THE SPINNAKER TOWER 2005 P100714k

SOUTHSEA, THE 'D' DAY MEMORIAL c1955 S161059

Drunken troops, mainly Irish, fired live ammunition at worshippers in the parish church, killing some and severely wounding others, during the chaotic weeks of October 1688, before King James II fled the country and the Glorious Revolution put William and Mary on the throne.

By the end of the 17th century, Portsmouth was the most strongly defended town in the country and was the leading naval dockyard.

The arsonist James Aitken, or 'Jack the Painter', as he was popularly known, was an ardent supporter of the ideals of the American revolutionaries. He tried to burn down the dockyard in 1776-7. He was finally caught and hanged outside the main dockyard gate.

Another advocate of the American cause was Thomas Wren, the minister of the High Street Presbyterian Chapel. He gave sanctuary to American seamen who had managed to escape from local prisons and arranged their passage, often in disguise, to London and further, usually to France.

Marc Brunel's steam-driven block-making machinery, introduced into Portsmouth Dockyard in 1801, was the first example in the world of the use of metal machines for mass-production.

There is a remarkable collection of material relating to Portsmouth in the Turner Bequest in Tate Britain. J M W Turner visited the town at least four times and on each occasion he kept a sketchbook. Even today, the little line drawings are of clearly recognisable local scenes and places. Southsea Castle, the defences at the harbour entrance, St Thomas's, the dockyard and Gunwharf are particularly featured.

PORTSMOUTH, THE HARD 1890 22751

SOUTHSEA, THE BEACH AND PIER 1898 42693

Portsmouth dockyard trebled in size from 99 to 261 acres between the middle and the end of the 19th century. The mid 19th century Great Extension was the last great territorial expansion of the dockyard and, like all previous expansions in earlier centuries, was once again driven by fears of French military ambitions.

Portsmouth Theatre was immortalised in Charles Dickens's novel, 'Nicholas Nickleby', in which the eponymous hero and his companion, Smike, join Mr Vincent Crummles's theatrical company and perform there.

Portsmouth hosted a remarkable gathering of European leaders between 22 and 24 June 1814. This was the Visit of the Allied Sovereigns, to mark and celebrate what all believed was the end of hostilities against France. The Prince Regent presided over a gathering which included the King of Prussia,

the Emperor of Russia, the Duke of Wellington and Marshal Blucher. The guests, their retinues and the people of Portsmouth gave themselves up to three days of glorious celebrations.

PORTSMOUTH, HMS 'DUKE OF WELLINGTON' 1890 22755

PORTSMOUTH, THE BRITTANY FERRIES' SHIP, 'MONT ST MICHEL' 2005 P100709k

During the visit of the Allied Sovereigns in 1814, Marshal Blucher actually put up at the Crown Inn in the High Street with his accompanying staff.

It is not generally known that when Lord Nelson breakfasted at the George Hotel, on the morning of 14 September 1805, the crowds outside in the High Street were so great that he had to slip out through the back of the building into Penny Street. He made his way on foot down to the beach and, with Captain Hardy, threaded his way past the bathing machines and down to his boat.

Quebec House in Bath Square, Old Portsmouth is an early bathing house, built in the mid 18th century when the benefits of bathing in seawater were gaining currency. The bathing house was built by popular subscription. Some of its ground floor rooms still have trapdoors, through which bathers descended to the shingle and the saltwater beneath. Today, Quebec House is a private residence.

The man responsible for developing the elegant villas and terraces of early Southsea, a local architect and entrepreneur, lived at Dovercourt, Kent Road, now Portsmouth High School Junior School.

Portsmouth's fortifications were not demolished until the 1870s. The land released was used for a public park, Victoria Park, for playing fields for the naval and military personnel and for barracks. The City Museum and Records Office is housed in the one remaining block of the former Victoria and Clarence Barracks complex.

The railway line was built over the stretch of canal from Fratton Station to Portsmouth and Southsea Station. Goldsmith Avenue follows the route of the waterway from Milton to Fratton.

There have been four purpose-built town halls in Portsmouth: the 16th century building in the centre of the High Street opposite the Dolphin; its early 18th-century replacement; the early 19th century town hall next door to the Dolphin; and today's Guildhall, opened in 1890 and rebuilt after the Second World War, opening again in 1958. The Civic Offices were opened in 1974.

The Blue Posts Hotel in Broad Street was so-called because of the brightly-painted blue posts which flanked the entrance to the bar areas and the yard at the back of the building.

PORTSMOUTH, CHARLES II'S MARRIAGE CERTIFICATE ZZZ04527 (courtesy of Portsmouth Cathedral)

SOUTHSEA, WESTERN PARADE 1898 42690

Portsmouth Cathedral was extended twice in the course of the 20th century. Work began before the Second World War to enlarge the building to a size commensurate with its status as the cathedral church of the new Anglican diocese of Portsmouth. The outbreak of war in 1939 put a stop to the work and a single-skin red brick wall was hastily put up at the west end of the half-completed nave. The project was completed finally in the 1980s in the spirit of the original intentions of Sir Charles Nicholson.

Portsmouth possesses one of the finest collections of civic plate in the country. It includes several pieces acquired in the 16th century as well as a priceless collection of early 17th-century silver and silver-gilt standing cups.

Arthur Conan Doyle wrote the first Sherlock Holmes novel in Southsea in 1886.

ALVERSTOKE, THE CRESCENT 1898 42721

There were fourteen breweries in Portsmouth in 1902. By the end of the century there were none.

By 1939, the population of Portsmouth had risen to just over 250,000 people and the city's boundaries had reached their furthest extent, now embracing the mainland areas of Cosham, Paulsgrove and Wymering, Drayton and parts of Portchester.

The Guildhall was reduced to a smoking ruin by enemy air raids on the night of 10-11 January 1941, but the city's historic records and the priceless collection of civic plate survived the disaster in the basement of the Guildhall, being in a strongroom built by the security firm Chubb, who were themselves founded in Portsmouth in the 18th century.

The Guildhall might have survived the blitz of 10-11 January 1941 but for the fact that the water mains were also shattered that night and there was no water to put out the fires once they had gained a hold.

During the Second World War, Eisenhower's headquarters were at Southwick House, just outside Portsmouth, and it was there that he gave the historic 'order to go', which launched one of the greatest invasion offensives ever, to recapture Western Europe from Hitler's Germany - D-Day.

HAVANT c1900 H147099

PORTSMOUTH, THE DEVICE ZZZ04533 (from W G Gates,'Portsmouth in the Past')

Portsmouth in the Past

BY

WILLIAM G. GATES.

. . . . . .

Topographical Notes and Sketches
reprinted from the
"Hampshire Telegraph," 1925

—

PORTSMOUTH :
CHARPENTIER Ltd., 46, HIGH STREET.
1926.

Portmouth was the centre of the 'D-Day 50' Commemorations in 1994 and, as in 1814, the city was the venue for a remarkable assembly of heads of the allied states, including the Presidents of the United States and of France. HM the Queen held a glittering banquet for her guests in the Guildhall and a Drumhead Service was held on Southsea Common the following day.

PORTSMOUTH, TRAMS AT CLARENCE PIER ZZZ04520 (Portsmouth City Museums and Records Service)

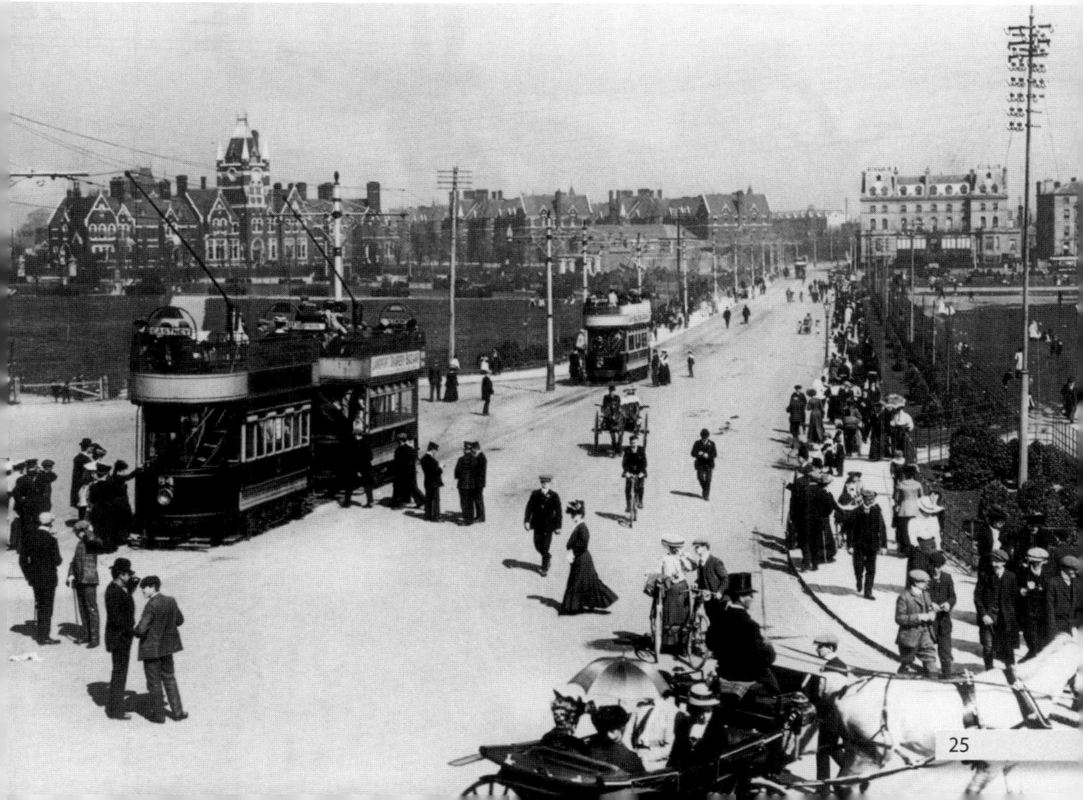

Portsmouth had a considerable corset industry in the 19th and early 20th centuries. There was a plentiful female labour force, many of whose menfolk were away at sea, so it was possible to keep wages low. Corsets were worn by men and women and several thousand women were employed in the trade, working either in their own homes or in local factories in the 19th century.

Portsmouth is the largest fruit-importing port in the country.

PORTSMOUTH, THE EMIGRANTS' STATUE 2005 P100720k

SOUTHSEA, SUSSEX TERRACE ZZZ04511 (Author's Collection)

PORTSMOUTH, BROAD STREET 2005 P100719k

The Gunwharf was Portsmouth's arsenal. Here the ordnance was kept, not only for ships, but also for the defences in general. There had been, from the 16th century, a gunwharf where ships unloaded their guns before they went into dock and picked them up on their way back to sea again.

Portsmouth Football Club won the FA Cup Final in 1939. Fixtures were suspended on the outbreak of war and the FA Cup was stowed away for the duration of the war, which is why Portsmouth can claim to have held the cup longer than any other football club.

Portsmouth's nickname is Pompey. It is not the prerogative of the football club to call itself by this name. The town, too, is known the world over as Pompey, but no one is very sure why. The most plausible reason relates to the story of the Portsmouth-based sailors who scaled Pompey's pillar in Alexandria in 1781 and toasted their success from the top with punch. Their efforts earned them the nickname 'the Pompey Boys'.

PORTSMOUTH QUIZ QUESTIONS

1. What is the name of the island on which Portsmouth stands?

2. On which side of Portsmouth is Langstone Harbour?

3. What is the name of the chalk outlier of the South Downs to the north of Portsmouth?

4. What does 'sudewede' - the old name for Portsmouth - mean?

5. What evidence was found of human activity in the greater Portsmouth area in the Palaeolithic Age?

PORTSMOUTH UNIVERSITY LABORATORIES 2005 P100712k

ALVERSTOKE, THE VILLAGE c1960 A42014

6. What changes happened in the greater Portsmouth area when the last Ice Age ended?

7. Why are the immigrants to Portsmouth around the time of the third millenium BC known as the 'Beaker' people?

8. Two Bronze Age hoards have been discovered on Portsea Island. On what sites?

9. Four of the first examples of coinage in Britain were found near Portsmouth. What age did they date from?

SOUTHSEA, THE ROCK GARDENS c1955 S161023

10. Who built Portchester Castle in the late 3rd century?

11. According to the Anglo-Saxon Chronicle, who came to Portsmouth in AD 501?

12. What are the names of the three pre-Conquest manors on Portsea Island?

13. What was the name of the French merchant and landowner who founded the new township of Portsmouth at the harbour mouth?

14. Where do the first references occur to Jean de Gisors and Portsmouth?

15. When did Jean de Gisors forfeit his Portsmouth property?

PORTSMOUTH, THE MEMORIAL TO THE DUKE OF BUCKINGHAM IN THE CATHEDRAL

ZZZ04526 (courtesy of Portsmouth Cathedral)

GOSPORT, FROM PORTSMOUTH c1965 G37109

16. What is the device on Portsmouth's common seal?

17. When did the first French raid on Portsmouth take place in the Hundred Years' War?

18. Who commissioned the building of the Square Tower?

19. What were the names of the four new brewhouses constructed in Portsmouth in 1512-13?

20. Where was Southsea Castle built?

21. When did the 'Mary Rose' sink?

22. Who was assassinated in Portsmouth in 1628?

23. Which local building was badly damaged during the Civil War?

24. Whom did King Charles II marry in Portsmouth in 1662?

SOUTHSEA, VICTORIA BARRACKS 1898 42698

PORTSMOUTH, PORT SOLENT 2005 P100708k

25. What was the gift given to Charles II and his bride by the people of Portsmouth?

26. What was the name of the military engineer who updated Portsmouth's defences in the 1660s?

27. Where was the baby Prince of Wales lodged in 1688, just before his father, James II, fled the country?

28. Whose action saved Portsmouth from chaos and confusion in late December 1688 during the turmoil surrounding the Glorious Revolution?

SOUTHSEA, THE ANCHOR OF HMS 'VICTORY' c1955 S161042

SOUTHSEA, THE ENTRANCE TO THE CASTLE 2005 S161702k

29. How many people worked in the dockyard in 1687?

30. When was the original dockyard church built and to whom is it dedicated?

31. What was the invention of Marc Brunel, which was installed in Portsmouth dockyard?

32. When did the composer Joseph Haydn visit Portsmouth?

33. Lord Palmerston was responsible for building a string of forts along the top of Portsdown. What are they called?

34. The new suburb of Portsea developed on land to the north of the original town. What was it called?

35. To whom did the inhabitants of Portsea dedicate their first church?

36. Who composed the overture 'Portsmouth Point' and when?

37. Where did Lord Nelson have his breakfast on 14 September 1805?

38. When did the first convict fleet sail from Portsmouth for New South Wales?

39. Where was the author Charles Dickens born?

40. What was the name of the company which brought the railway to Portsmouth in 1847?

PORTSMOUTH, THE CATHEDRAL EXTENSION ZZZ04531 (courtesy of Portsmouth Cathedral)

SOUTHSEA, THE MINIATURE RAILWAY c1955 S161060

41. When did Portsmouth become a city?

42. When was the Anglican diocese created?

43. What is the city's motto?

44. When was the Guildhall destroyed in the Second World War?

45. Who designed Brickwood's distinctive half-timbered public houses?

SOUTHSEA, A HOVERCRAFT ON THE SEAFRONT 2005 S161704k

46. What was the name of Portsmouth's oldest hospital?

PORTSMOUTH HARBOUR AND HMS 'VICTORY' 1890 22754

A PLAN OF PORTSMOUTH ZZZ04523 (W G Gates, 'Portsmouth in the Past')

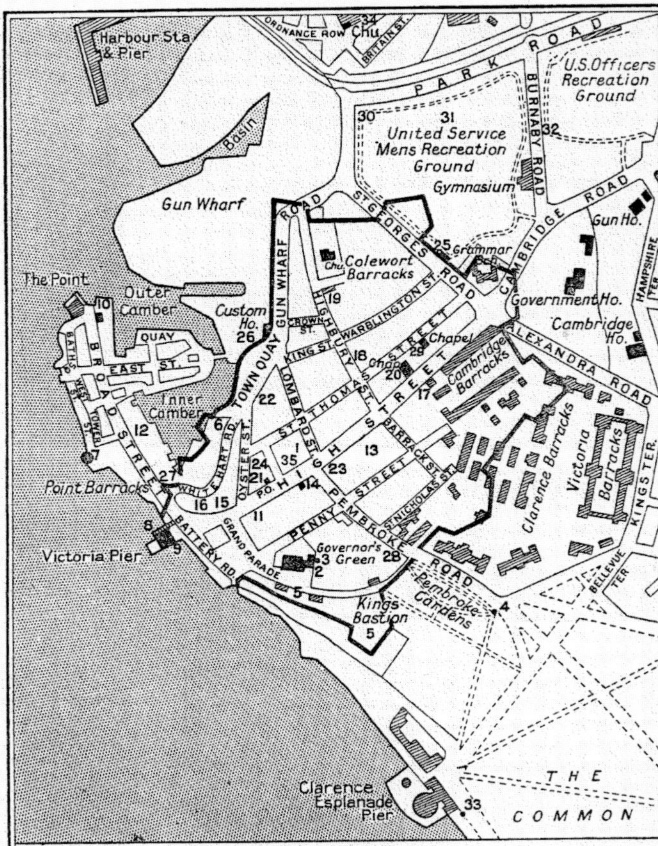

REFERENCE.

1 Church of St. Thomas a Becket.
2 Garrison Church, old Domus Dei.
3 Old Mortar on Governor's Green.
4 "Royal George" Gun.
5 Old Fortifications remaining.
6 Old Fortifications remaining.
7 The Round Tower.
8 The Sally Port.
9 Old Semaphore Tower.
10 "Star & Garter" Hotel.
11 Old "Fountain" Hotel (now Soldiers Institute).
12 Old "Blue Posts" Inn.
13 The "George" Hotel.
14 The Museum.
15 Admiral Anson's House.
16 House where George Meredith was born.
17 House where the Duke of Buckingham was assassinated.
18 Admiral Lord Howe's House.
19 John Pound's House.
20 John Pound's Burial Place & Monument.
21 Chapel where John Wesley preached.
22 Old "Globe" Hotel—famous coaching ho.
23 Site of "Crown" Hotel.
24 Site of "Red Lion" Hotel.
25 Landport Gate.
26 The Quay Gate.
27 King James' Gate.
28 King William's Gate.
29 Admiral Palisser's House.
30 Kings Mill.
31 Mill Pond.
32 Mill Dam.
33 Where the Gibbet stood.
34 St. George's Church.
35 Site of "Three Tuns" Hotel
—— Line of Fortifications.

Copyright Charpentier & Co. Portsmouth

47. Who founded Portsmouth Grammar School?

48. What was the colour of Portsmouth Football Club's original kit?

PORTSMOUTH, MILTON 2005 P100723k

49. Which team did Portsmouth Football Club beat to win the FA Cup in 1939?

50. What was the name of the French warship which was captured in 1793, taken into the British fleet and finished its days as a guard ship in Portsmouth?

PORTSMOUTH, THE ENTHRONEMENT OF THE FIRST BISHOP

ZZZ04529 (courtesy of Portsmouth Cathedral)

SOUTHSEA, THE CANOE LAKE c1955 S161049

PORTSMOUTH QUIZ ANSWERS

1. Portsea Island.

2. The east side.

3. Portsdown.

4. South wade or water.

5. Hand axes and flint blades.

6. The landscape evolved to forests.

7. Because they were buried beneath a round barrow with a tall pottery vessel called a beaker.

8. The sites of St Mary's Hospital and St James's Hospital.

9. c150 BC.

10. Carausius, to help protect Roman Britain from North Sea pirates.

11. Port and his two sons, Bieda and Maegla.

12. Buckland, Copnor and Fratton.

13. Jean de Gisors.

14. The Southwick Cartularies.

15. 1194.

16. A ship with castle and furled sail, with a crescent on the left of the mast and a star on the right.

17. 1339.

18. Henry VII.

19. The Rose, the Lion, the Dragon and the White Hart.

20. Ketes Point.

21. 18 July 1545.

22. The Duke of Buckingham.

23. The parish church, St Thomas's.

24. Catherine of Braganza.

25. A silver and crystal salt-cellar.

26. Sir Bernard de Gomme.

27. Alderman Ridge's house in the High Street.

28. Colonel Richard Norton of Southwick, who raised the country to bring in reinforcements to protect the town from the disaffected troops, mainly Irish, who had been loyal to James II and had now been dismissed from their regiments and were roaming the area.

29. 294.

30. It was built in 1704, and was dedicated to St Ann.

31. Pulley-block making machinery.

32. 1794. He was not allowed to visit the dockyard because he was a foreigner.

33. Wallington, Nelson, Southwick, Widley, Purbrook and Farlington.

34. Portsmouth Common and the east and west Dock Fields.

35. St George.

36. Sir William Walton composed this piece in 1925.

37. The George Hotel in the High Street.

38. 1787.

39. 393, Commercial Road.

40. The London, Brighton and South Coast railway.

41. 1926.

42. 1927.

43. Heaven's Light our Guide.

44. 10-11 January 1941.

45. A E Cogswell.

46. The Royal Portsmouth Hospital.

47. Dr William Smith.

48. Salmon pink.

49. Wolves (4 - 1).

50. La Pompee.

GOUDHURST, MEASURING THE HOPS 1904 52571

GENERAL HISTORY QUIZ QUESTIONS

1. Which 20th-century Prime Minister was a proficient bricklayer and a member of the union?

2. In Victorian times, what powerful substance did many fashionable society ladies use to spice up their afternoon tea parties?

3. What was the first battle of the English Civil War on 23 October 1642?

4. Who was Queen Victoria's first Prime Minister?

5. Which Michigan-born dentist was arrested in Canada for the murder of his wife in London?

6. For what crime was Titus Oates pilloried in the stocks and flogged every year?

7. What crime was committed by Burke and Hare?

8. What language was Elizabeth I not fluent in? German, French, Latin, or Italian?

9. In 1834 six Dorset farm labourers were transported to Australia. By what name are these men usually known?

HORNING, ON THE BROADS 1902 48108

MARKET DRAYTON, MARKET DAY 1911 63338

10. At which battle was Richard III slain?

11. Who was the first Prime Minister to live at Chequers?

12. Who was the leader of the Women's Social and Political Union?

13. In which year were women granted the vote on the Isle of Man? 1881, 1902, 1912, or 1946?

RHYL, DONKEYS ON THE SANDS 1891 29151

14. Which king signed the Magna Carta in 1215 at Runnymede?

15. In which city was the infamous Peterloo Massacre on 16 August 1819?

16. Who were the mother and father of Elizabeth I?

17. Before the French Revolution in 1789, who is reported to have said 'Let them eat cake'?

18. Who wore two shirts in which to be executed, and why?

SHANKLIN, THE STAGECOACHES 1913 66211A

NEWQUAY, THE HARBOUR 1894 33522

19. Which queen was known as Bloody Mary?

20. Who was the only English pope?

21. Which British king married May of Teck?

22. At the outbreak of World War I, who was the British Prime Minister?

23. What great structure, designed by Joseph Paxton, was built in 1851?

24. What were the names of the two princes believed to have been murdered in the Tower of London in 1483?

25. What unusual accident eventually caused the death of the Prince of Wales, eldest son of George II?

26. Which of Dickens's novels depicts the struggles and strife of factory workers in Victorian England?

EVERSLEY, THE WHITE HART 1906 57011

CASTLETON, SPEEDWELL CAVERN 1909 61785

27. How old was William Shakespeare when he got married? 24, 25, 19, or 18?

28. What crime occurred on 8 August 1963 that shocked public opinion in Britain?

29. Who had to hide in an oak tree to save his life after a military defeat?

30. After Henry VIII's Dissolution of the Monasteries, what are some of the new owners of the monastery buildings rumoured to have done with some of the illuminated manuscripts they found?

KING'S LYNN, HIGH STREET 1908 60023

BOURNEMOUTH, INVALID'S WALK 1900 45226

31. In July 1888, 1,500 female employees went on strike at a factory at Bow in East London. What did they manufacture?

32. Who was the Irish saint who legend says saw the Loch Ness Monster in Scotland?
St Columba, St Patrick, St Andrew, or St Aidan?

33. Which English woman made this prophecy:
'Carriages without horses shall go, And accidents fill the world with woe. Around the world thoughts shall fly, In the twinkling of an eye.'?

34. Which tax was levied between 1696 and 1851?

35. How long did the Hundred Years' War last? 116 years, 94 years, 100 years, or 108 years?

36. Who was called the 'Old Pretender'?

37. In 1629 William Harvey published the details of a discovery he had made. What was it?

38. Put these wars and battles in the order in which they took place:
A. The Battle of Agincourt
B. The Battle of Hastings
C. Marston Moor
D. Wars of the Roses

39. In British army slang, what was a 'dead man'?

40. When was the Poll Tax first introduced in England?

SAFFRON WALDEN, FRY'S GARDEN 1907 S58821

CLOVELLY, POST OFFICE, TRANSFER OF MAIL 1936 87551

41. Who was the first Prime Minister of Britain?

42. What is pannage?

43. What were the Welshmen of the Rebecca Riots, who dressed up as women, protesting against?

44. How many people did the 1715 Riot Act have to be read to, in order for them to be guilty of a felony, and liable to the punishment of death? 6, 12, 27, or 250?

CHALFORD, THE VILLAGE 1910 62713

45. What was the joint stock company, the South Sea Company, set up in 1711 to trade in?

46. In the Middle Ages, a split stick was used by royal officials to record sums of money paid. Notches were cut on it representing payments. What was it called?

EASTBOURNE, THE PIER 1925 77946

WEYMOUTH, THE SANDS 1909 61597

47. When did the Union Jack achieve its present pattern?

48. In 1752, September 2 was followed by September 14. What was the name of the new calendar system that involved this adjustment?

NEWBY BRIDGE, THE SWAN HOTEL 1914 67414

49. Coffee houses were patronised by literary giants such as Dryden, Johnson, and Pope. How many coffee houses were there in London in the 18th century?
10, 50, 250, or 1800?

50. Who was the first British Prime Minister to live at 10 Downing Street?

TENBY 1890 28091

GENERAL HISTORY QUIZ ANSWERS

1. Winston Churchill.

2. Opium.

3. Edgehill.

4. Lord Melbourne.

5. Dr Crippen. He buried her body in the basement of his London house.

6. For giving false evidence against Catholics.

7. They murdered people and sold their corpses to unscrupulous surgeons for dissection.

8. German.

9. The Tolpuddle Martyrs.

10. The Battle of Bosworth Field.

11. Lloyd George.

12. Emmeline Pankhurst.

13. 1881.

14. King John.

15. Manchester.

16. Henry VIII and Anne Boleyn.

17. Marie Antoinette.

18. Charles I. The weather was cold and he did not want to be seen shivering.

19. Mary I, the daughter of Henry VIII and Catherine of Aragon. She married Philip II of Spain, and was a devout Catholic. She earned her nickname from her persecution of Protestants.

20. Adrian IV, born Nicholas Brakespeare in 1100.

21. George V (she was known in this country as Mary).

22. Herbert Asquith.

23. The Crystal Palace.

24. Edward V and his brother Richard Duke of York, the sons of Edward IV.

25. He was hit on the head by a cricket ball.

GENERAL HISTORY QUIZ ANSWERS

26. 'Hard Times', published in 1854.

27. 18.

28. The Great Train Robbery.

29. Charles II.

30. They used them as lavatory paper.

31. Matches. They worked at the Bryant and May factory.

32. St Columba, born cAD521.

33. Mother Shipton, born in Norfolk in 1485.

34. Window Tax, which was payable on a house with more than six windows.

35. 116 years, between 1337 and 1453.

36. James III (the son of James II). In 1715 he gathered together a force of 10,000 men and invaded England. The Jacobites fought their way as far as Preston, where they were dispersed.

37. The circulation of the blood. He was physician extraordinary to James I.

38. B (1066) A (1415) D (1455-85) C (1644).

39. An empty bottle.

40. In 1222, on every person over the age of 14.

41. Robert Walpole. As first Lord of the Treasury between 1721 and 1742 he presided over the cabinet.

42. The right of tenants to graze their swine in the woods of a manor.

43. They destroyed turnpike houses, being unhappy about the levels of tolls.

44. 12.

45. Slaves in Latin America.

46. A tally.

47. In 1801, when the cross of St Patrick was added to the crosses of St George and St Andrew.

48. The Gregorian Calendar.

49. 1800.

50. Sir Robert Walpole (1676-1745).

FRANCIS FRITH

PIONEER VICTORIAN PHOTOGRAPHER

Francis Frith, founder of the world-famous photographic archive, was a complex and multi-talented man. A devout Quaker and a highly successful Victorian businessman, he was philosophical by nature and pioneering in outlook. By 1855 he had already established a wholesale grocery business in Liverpool, and sold it for the astonishing sum of £200,000, which is the equivalent today of over £15,000,000. Now in his thirties, and captivated by the new science of photography, Frith set out on a series of pioneering journeys up the Nile and to the Near East.

INTRIGUE AND EXPLORATION

He was the first photographer to venture beyond the sixth cataract of the Nile. Africa was still the mysterious 'Dark Continent', and Stanley and Livingstone's historic meeting was a decade into the future. The conditions for picture taking confound belief. He laboured for hours in his wicker dark-room in the sweltering heat of the desert, while the volatile chemicals fizzed dangerously in their trays. Back in London he exhibited his photographs and was 'rapturously cheered' by members of the Royal Society. His reputation as a photographer was made overnight.

VENTURE OF A LIFE-TIME

By the 1870s the railways had threaded their way across the country, and Bank Holidays and half-day Saturdays had been made obligatory by Act of Parliament. All of a sudden the working man and his family were able to enjoy days out, take holidays, and see a little more of the world.

With typical business acumen, Francis Frith foresaw that these new tourists would enjoy having souvenirs to commemorate their days out. For the next thirty years he travelled the country by train and by pony and trap, producing fine photographs of seaside resorts and beauty spots that were keenly bought by millions of Victorians. These prints were painstakingly pasted into family albums and pored over during the dark nights of winter, rekindling precious memories of summer excursions. Frith's studio was soon supplying retail shops all over the country, and by 1890 F Frith & Co had become the greatest specialist photographic publishing company in the world, with over 2,000 sales outlets, and pioneered the picture postcard.

FRANCIS FRITH'S LEGACY

Francis Frith had died in 1898 at his villa in Cannes, his great project still growing. By 1970 the archive he created contained over a third of a million pictures showing 7,000 British towns and villages.

Frith's legacy to us today is of immense significance and value, for the magnificent archive of evocative photographs he created provides a unique record of change in the cities, towns and villages throughout Britain over a century and more. Frith and his fellow studio photographers revisited locations many times down the years to update their views, compiling for us an enthralling and colourful pageant of British life and character.

We are fortunate that Frith was dedicated to recording the minutiae of everyday life. For it is this sheer wealth of visual data, the painstaking chronicle of changes in dress, transport, street layouts, buildings, housing and landscape that captivates us so much today, offering us a powerful link with the past and with the lives of our ancestors.

Computers have now made it possible for Frith's many thousands of images to be accessed almost instantly. The archive offers every one of us an opportunity to examine the places where we and our families have lived and worked down the years. Its images, depicting our shared past, are now bringing pleasure and enlightenment to millions around the world a century and more after his death.

For further information visit: www.francisfrith.co.uk

FRITH PRODUCTS & SERVICES

Francis Frith would doubtless be pleased to know that the pioneering publishing venture he started in 1860 still continues today. Over a hundred and forty years later, The Francis Frith Collection continues in the same innovative tradition and is now one of the foremost publishers of vintage photographs in the world. Some of the current activities include:

INTERIOR DECORATION

Today Frith's photographs can be seen framed and as giant wall murals in thousands of pubs, restaurants, hotels, banks, retail stores and other public buildings throughout the country. In every case they enhance the unique local atmosphere of the places they depict and provide reminders of gentler days in an increasingly busy and frenetic world.

PRODUCT PROMOTIONS

Frith products are used by many major companies to promote the sales of their own products or to reinforce their own history and heritage. Frith promotions have been used by Hovis bread, Courage beers, Scots Porage Oats, Colman's mustard, Cadbury's foods, Mellow Birds coffee, Dunhill pipe tobacco, Guinness, and Bulmer's Cider.

GENEALOGY AND FAMILY HISTORY

As the interest in family history and roots grows world-wide, more and more people are turning to Frith's photographs of Great Britain for images of the towns, villages and streets where their ancestors lived; and, of course, photographs of the churches and chapels where their ancestors were christened, married and buried are an essential part of every genealogy tree and family album.

FRITH PRODUCTS

All Frith photographs are available Framed or just as Mounted Prints and Posters (size 23 x 16 inches). These may be ordered from the address below. From time to time other products - Address Books, Calendars, Table Mats, etc - are available.

THE INTERNET

Already one hundred thousand Frith photographs can be viewed and purchased on the internet through the Frith websites and a myriad of partner sites.

For more detailed information on Frith companies and products, look at these sites:

www.francisfrith.co.uk

www.francisfrith.com

(for North American Visitors)

See the complete list of Frith Books at:

www.francisfrith.co.uk

This web site is regularly updated with the latest list of publications from The Francis Frith Collection. If you wish to buy books relating to another part of the country that your local bookshop does not stock, you may purchase on-line.

For further information, trade, or author enquiries please contact us at the address below:

The Francis Frith Collection, Frith's Barn, Teffont, Salisbury, Wiltshire, England SP3 5QP.

Tel: +44 (0)1722 716 376 Fax: +44 (0)1722 716 881

e-mail: sales@francisfrith.co.uk

See all Frith products on the internet at www.francisfrith.co.uk